Jump Rope

by

Lisa Brown

First published in the UK in 2013 by Red Kite Books,
an imprint of Haldane Mason Ltd
PO Box 34196, London NW10 3YB
www.redkitebooks4kids.com

Copyright © Haldane Mason Ltd, 2013

ISBN: 978-1-905339-81-5

Printed in China

9 7 5 3 1 2 4 6 8

Illustrations by Jane Smith

Picture acknowledgements:
The picture on page 4 is reproduced from
a print published in England in 1800.
Corbis: page 5.

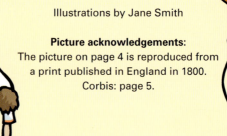

Contents

Where it all began . . .

No one seems to know the exact origin of jumping rope (or skipping, as it is also known in some parts of the world). Some people think that it dates back to rope-making in ancient Egypt or China. Others think it may have come from an Ancient Greek game where two people held a pole for another to jump over. Another theory is that the aborigines in Australia jumped with jungle vines.

These ideas and games were probably brought back to Europe by sailors, and images of children jumping rope in the streets appear in some Medieval European paintings. Rope skipping was taken to America by Dutch settlers during the 1600s, and it has spread steadily ever since. By the late twentieth century, the skipping rope or jump rope was a common sight in many children's playgrounds around the world, and it is now used by many adults, too.

An English pin-up print from 1800 – complete with skipping rope.

Jump rope is good for you!

Jumping rope is a great activity that has many benefits. Not only is it a fun recreation activity and an increasingly popular competitive sport, it also provides a complete cardiovascular workout, similar to running or cycling. You get about the same amount of exercise from ten minutes of jumping rope as you do from running an 8-minute mile. It's also better for your knees than jogging, as you land on the balls of your feet rather than your heels, causing less jarring.

In the late 1970s, the Jump Rope for Heart program emerged in the US.

More than anything, jump rope is fun!

This school fundraising program promotes healthy living through physical activity and is prevalent in elementary schools all over the USA.

Today, the benefits of jump rope are universally recognized. It is used all over the world as a method of cross-training for numerous sports, including boxing, westling, and tennis. Jump rope appeared for the first time at the London Olympic Games in August 2012 as a demonstration during basketball match breaks – not yet as an Olympic sport, but perhaps it will be one day soon!

Benefits of jump rope

- *It is one of the most complete full-body workouts, working many different muscle groups simultaneously.*
- *It increases lung capacity and the quality of the cardiovascular system.*
- *It increases endurance, flexibility, and muscular strength.*
- *It improves overall coordination and balance.*

Jump rope today

FISAC–IRSF (Fédération Internationale de Saut à la Corde– International Rope Skipping Federation) serves as the international governing body for the sport of jump rope. This organization hosts the World Championships every 2 years in a different host country. Host countries so far include Australia, Belgium, Canada, South Africa, South Korea, the UK, and the USA.

Europe, Asia, Africa, Canada, and the US all host tournaments to qualify athletes for the FISAC–IRSF World Championships. In addition to National and International competitions that are exclusively for jump ropers, Jump Rope is one of the sports included in the AAU (US Amateur Athletic Union) Junior Olympics each year.

In 1995, USA Jump Rope became the national governing body for the sport of Jump Rope in the United States. USA Jump Rope is a non-profit organization that hosts regional and national competitions, workshops, performances, and camps with the goal of instilling healthy habits in people of all ages by growing the sport of jump rope. There are now similar bodies in other countries, such as the ERSO (European Rope Skipping Organisation), ARSA (African Rope Skipping Association), ARSF (Asian Rope Skipping Federation), and ORSA (Oceania Rope Skipping Association).

Jump Rope is gradually making its way into the media spotlight. The USA Jump Rope National Tournament has been broadcast on TV. Teams around the world do performances for local news stations, basketball half times, commercials, and movie cameos. There is also a US National All Star Team that travels to do high profile performances. Get Tricky, an international jump rope team, performed for the first time at the London Olympic Games in 2012. Recently, three jump rope groups competed on talent-based reality shows. Saltare was a jump rope crew on MTV's America's Best Dance Crew. Summerwind Skippers competed on NBC's America's Got Talent. A Double Dutch group from Belgium, DDF, won Holland's Got Talent. As the sport receives more media exposure, so it becomes more and more popular.

Single rope competition events

Competition events tend to be split into two main categories, Speed and Freestyle.

Speed events

For speed events, judges count how many times an athlete can jump the rope in a given amount of time. The most common Single Rope Speed Events are:

Fun Fact:
The judges only count every other jump because the jumpers jump too fast for the judges to count each one. The judges double the score at the end to show how many jumps the athlete completed in the allotted time.

Individual Single Rope Speed
Using the Jogging Step (page 22), you must complete as many jumps as you can in 30 seconds, 1 minute, and 3 minutes.
Current World Record:
• 30 seconds: 204 jumps
• 3 minutes: 1,000 jumps

Individual Single Rope Double Unders
You must complete as many Double Unders (page 32) as you can in 30 seconds and 1 minute.

Consecutive Triple Unders
This event is not timed. You must do as many straight Triple Unders

(where the rope passes under your feet 3 times before landing – page 46) as you can without making an error or taking any extra jumps between each Triple Under.
Current World Record:
450 Triple Unders

Single Rope Speed Relay
This event requires a team of four people. Using the Jogging Step, each member of the team must complete as many jumps as he or she can in 30 seconds. Only one person jumps at a time. The event lasts 2 minutes.

Introduction

7

Freestyle events

For freestyle events, competitors are judged by a panel on the difficulty, density, creativity, and presentation of their routines. Making an error results in marks being deducted. For team events, competitors are also judged on their synchronicity. Freestyle routines may be choreographed to music.

The most common Single Rope Freestyle Events are:

Individual Single Rope Freestyle

One person is judged on a routine lasting between 1 minute and 1 minute 15 seconds. The jumper puts tricks together in combinations to form a routine.

Pairs Single Rope Freestyle

Two people choreograph a routine to perform together. Most of the time both people will do the same tricks at the same time (in sync). They can also add in partner tricks like Scoops (page 54).

Fun Fact: Double Dutch is a jump rope game in which two long jump ropes are turned in opposite directions for one or more players to jump over at the same time. It is a major aspect of competition too. As this is a Single Rope manual, Double Dutch is not discussed… but it is not to be forgotten!

4-Person Team Freestyle

This event is similar to Pairs Freestyle, but is more advanced as it requires four people to be in sync instead of just two.

Team Show

A team of between six and 30 people are judged on a choreographed routine that lasts between 3 and 5 minutes. It may include many different tricks, although Single Rope Freestyle, Traveller (page 62), and Wheel (page 60) are the most common.

Sizing your rope

It is very important that you use a rope that is the correct size for you. If your rope is too short, it won't be able to clear your head or your feet and you will have a greater chance of making a mistake. If your rope is too long, it will drag on the floor and it will be difficult to control properly.

Ideal rope length is not solely based on height – it is also a matter of individual preference. Some people prefer their rope to be slightly longer, others like a shorter rope. Try different lengths until you find what suits you.

Your handles should come up just below your armpits. They should never be higher than your armpits or lower than your waist. You can try different sizes to see what works best for you.

To get a general idea of what size rope you should use, follow these simple instructions:
1. Hold your rope with one handle in each hand.
2. Step on the middle of the rope and pull your arms up so the rope is tight.

Proper Form

Using proper form will not only make the skills you are doing look better, it will also make the skills easier.

Your arms should always stay close to your sides. Your hands should stay low near your hips.

Yes   *No*

Stand tall with your back straight and your chest up.

Yes   *No*

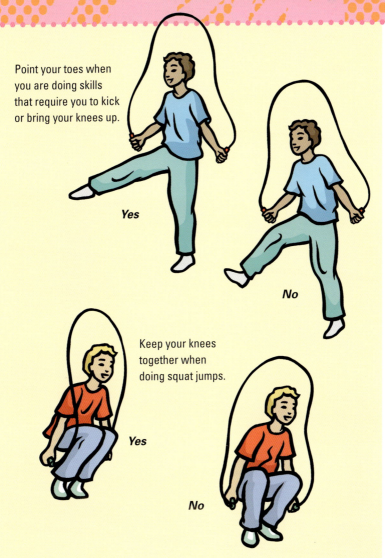

Point your toes when you are doing skills that require you to kick or bring your knees up.

Yes

No

Keep your knees together when doing squat jumps.

Yes

No

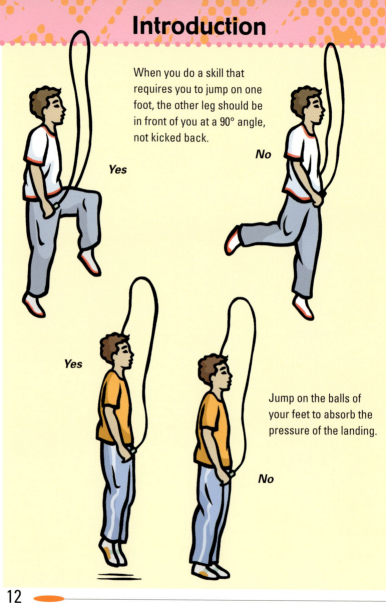

When you do a skill that requires you to jump on one foot, the other leg should be in front of you at a 90° angle, not kicked back.

Yes

No

Yes

Jump on the balls of your feet to absorb the pressure of the landing.

No

Fundamentals

Basic Bounce

1. Hold one handle of the rope in each hand and make sure you are standing in front of the rope.

2. With both arms moving at the same time, bring the rope up behind your back and over your head.

3. Continue to use your arms to bring the arc of the rope down in front of you to your feet.

Every time your feet leave the ground for a basic bounce, the rope should pass under your feet before you land.

4. Jump over the rope while still turning it. Continue to turn the rope so that it will pass over your head and come round to your feet again, when you jump it again.

Backwards Jump

1. Set up as if you were going to do a regular Basic Bounce, except this time you should stand behind the rope.

2. Bring the rope up in front of you and over your head by turning your arms in a backward circle.

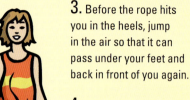

3. Before the rope hits you in the heels, jump in the air so that it can pass under your feet and back in front of you again.

4. Continue turning the rope in the backwards circle while you are jumping over it. At each turn, the rope should pass over your head and back down toward your heels for you to jump over.

Basic Sideswing

1. Set up with the rope in front of you as if you were going to do a Backwards Jump.

2. Put your right arm across your body and keep your left arm by your left side so that your hands are together and the rope turns directly to your left. Swing the rope so that it goes in a big circle above your head.

3. You can swing the rope on one side of your body or you can swing from one side to the other.

4. To move into a trick, simply bring your hand back across your body so that you can jump the rope.

Easy
Tricks

Criss-cross

1. Turn the rope over your head. Once it passes above your head, begin to cross your arms in front of your body. This should form a large loop for you to jump through.

Tip:
If the loop is not big enough for you to jump through, cross your arms further.

2. Keep your arms crossed until after you have jumped through the loop. Once you have jumped over the rope, continue turning it until it is over your head.

Challenge:
Once you can do one cross, try jumping multiple Criss-crosses in a row before uncrossing your arms.

3. After the rope passes over your head, uncross your arms and jump normally through the open loop.

Sideswing Cross

1. Start with a Basic Sideswing (page 14) to your right.

2. Continue to turn the rope. Once the arc is over your head, cross your right arm across your body while leaving your left arm on your right side.

3. Keep your arms crossed until after you have jumped through the loop. Once you have jumped over the rope, continue turning the rope until it is over your head.

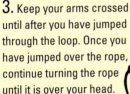

Tip: Make sure you can complete this skill with a Sideswing to the left AND to the right!

4. After the rope passes over your head, uncross your arms and jump through the open loop.

Easy Tricks

Overhead Swing

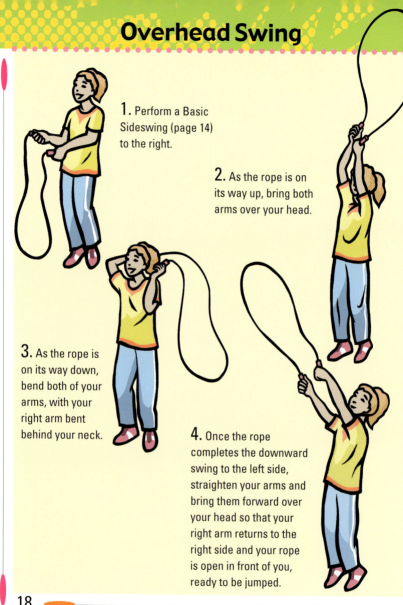

1. Perform a Basic Sideswing (page 14) to the right.

2. As the rope is on its way up, bring both arms over your head.

3. As the rope is on its way down, bend both of your arms, with your right arm bent behind your neck.

4. Once the rope completes the downward swing to the left side, straighten your arms and bring them forward over your head so that your right arm returns to the right side and your rope is open in front of you, ready to be jumped.

Skier, Bell

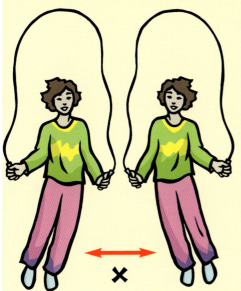

Skier

1. Jump over the rope, landing to the right of where your feet originally were.

2. On the next jump of the rope, land to the left of your original starting position.

3. Continue to alternate, jumping to the right and to the left.

Bell

1. Jump over your rope, landing in front of where your feet originally were.

2. On the next jump of the rope, land behind your original starting position.

3. Continue to alternate, jumping forward and backward.

Easy Tricks

Forward Straddle

1. Jump over your rope, landing with your right foot forward and your left foot back.

2. On the next jump of the rope, switch your feet, to place your left foot in front and your right foot back.

Side Straddle

1. On your first jump of the rope, land with your feet slightly wider than shoulder-width apart.

2. Bring your feet back together on the next jump.

Can-can

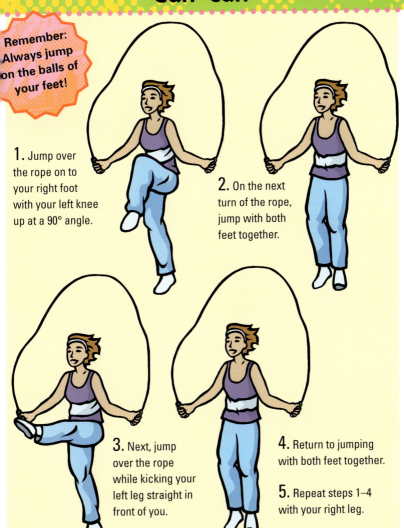

Remember: Always jump on the balls of your feet!

1. Jump over the rope on to your right foot with your left knee up at a 90° angle.

2. On the next turn of the rope, jump with both feet together.

3. Next, jump over the rope while kicking your left leg straight in front of you.

4. Return to jumping with both feet together.

5. Repeat steps 1–4 with your right leg.

Easy Tricks

Jogging Step

1. Begin turning the rope over your head. Jump on to your right foot as the rope passes underneath your feet. Your knee should be at a 90° angle to the ground.

Proper Form

Tip #1: *You should bring your knees UP instead of kicking your feet BACK.*

Tip #2: *Your arms should be slightly bent at the elbows and your wrists should turn in small circles.*

2. The next time the rope comes around, jump over it on to your left foot.

3. Continue to alternate feet with each pass of the rope.

Ready for a more difficult challenge?? Once you've mastered the jogging step, ask a friend to count how many you can do in 30 seconds.

This jogging step is the basis for many competitive speed events.

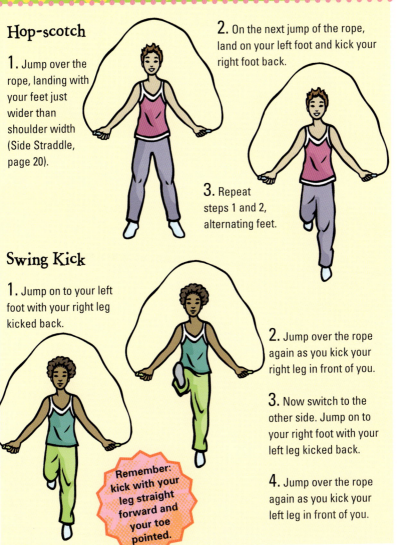

Hop-scotch

1. Jump over the rope, landing with your feet just wider than shoulder width (Side Straddle, page 20).

2. On the next jump of the rope, land on your left foot and kick your right foot back.

3. Repeat steps 1 and 2, alternating feet.

Swing Kick

1. Jump on to your left foot with your right leg kicked back.

2. Jump over the rope again as you kick your right leg in front of you.

3. Now switch to the other side. Jump on to your right foot with your left leg kicked back.

4. Jump over the rope again as you kick your left leg in front of you.

Remember: kick with your leg straight forward and your toe pointed.

Easy Tricks

Heel-to-toe, Fling

Heel-to-toe

1. On your first jump of the rope, touch your right heel out in front of you.

2. On your second jump , touch your right toe to the ground behind you.

3. Repeat steps 1 and 2 with your left leg.

Fling

1. Jump over the rope and tap your right toe behind you.

3. To complete the fling, touch your right heel out in front of you as you jump over the rope.

2. On the next jump of the rope, tap your right toe out to the right side of your body.

4. Repeat steps 1–3 with your left leg.

Spread Eagle, Russian Cossack

Spread Eagle

1. Jump down into a squat position.

2. Jump up to a standing position with your legs in the Straddle position (page 20).

3. Jump back down to the squat position on the next turn of the rope.

4. Repeat steps 2 and 3.

Russian Cossack

3. Repeat step 1.

1. Jump down into a squat position.

2. Jump back up as if you were doing the Spread Eagle, but land on just your left leg with your right leg kicked straight out in front of you.

4. Repeat step 2, but this time kick your left leg out. Continue, alternating legs. Remember to point your toes on the kicks.

Easy Tricks

Cross Over

1. On the first jump of the rope, bring your right knee up to your waist level.

2. On the next jump, cross your right leg over to touch your right toe to the ground on the left side of your body.

3. Return your knee up to waist height.

4. Complete the Cross Over by returning your right leg to the ground for a normal Basic Bounce (page 13).

5. Repeat steps 1 to 3 with your left leg.

Feel free to add your own variations. Instead of a regular knee-up jump, try throwing in a kick!

Beginner Push-up

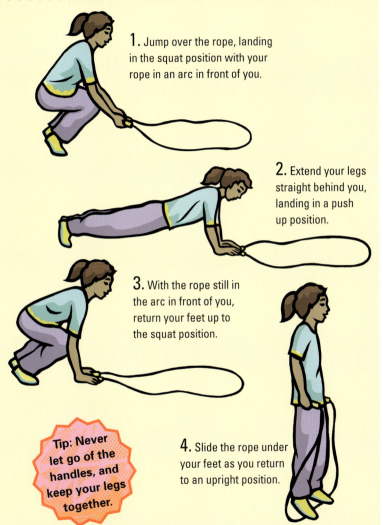

1. Jump over the rope, landing in the squat position with your rope in an arc in front of you.

2. Extend your legs straight behind you, landing in a push up position.

3. With the rope still in the arc in front of you, return your feet up to the squat position.

4. Slide the rope under your feet as you return to an upright position.

Tip: Never let go of the handles, and keep your legs together.

Easy Tricks

Beginner Frog

1. Place the rope in an arc in front of you as you kick up into a handstand.

2. Once your feet come together at the top of the handstand, bend your knees so your feet touch the backs of your legs.

Tip: The more upright you can land on step 3, the better.

3. Snap your feet back down to the ground, pushing off your hands at the same time.

4. Slide the rope under your feet as you jump to an upright position.

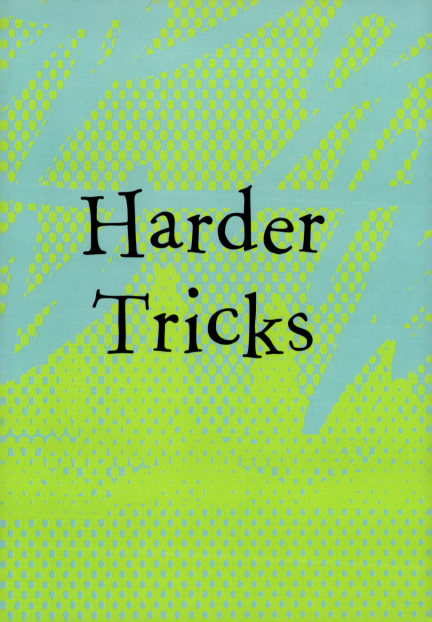

Harder Tricks

Single Handle Release

1. After you jump over the rope, let go of one of your rope handles.

Tip: Try to get the rope to lie in a straight line behind you.

2. Pull the rope straight forward with moderate strength. You may find it easier to take a step forward while pulling and use a bowling motion.

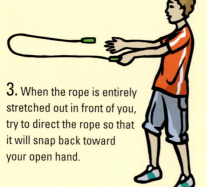

3. When the rope is entirely stretched out in front of you, try to direct the rope so that it will snap back toward your open hand.

Ready for a more difficult challenge? Once you are comfortable with catching the handle, try working it into other tricks – such as Criss-cross (page 16), 360° (page 37), Double Under (page 32), Crougar (page 34).

4. Catch the rope handle with your open hand, then continue jumping.

Arm Wraps

Basic Arm Wrap

1. As the rope comes over your head, cross one of your arms across your body to perform a Sideswing (page 14). If you swing to the right side of your body, your right handle should be furthest from you.

2. Stretch your right arm out to the side while you swing the rope again on the same side of your body. This should cause the the rope to wrap around your arm.

3. To unwrap the rope, swing the wrapped arm to the other side of your body. It may take more than one swing to completely unwrap the rope.

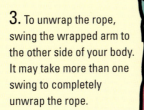

4. Once your arm is free of the rope, jump over the rope with your arms open.

180° Wrap

1. Complete Steps 1 and 2 of the Basic Arm Wrap (above).

2. To unwrap the rope, swing the rope to the opposite side of your body as you did in Step 3 of the Basic Arm Wrap. As the rope is hits the ground, turn your body 180° toward that side so you are facing backward.

3. Open up your arms and turn the rope over your head backward.

4. You should now be jumping the rope backwards.

Double Under

1. This trick is completed by jumping high and spinning the rope quickly so that it passes under your feet twice before you land.

2. If you are having trouble making it work, here are some tips:
- Spin your wrists in small, fast circles
- Keep your arms close to your body
- Bring your knees up to your chest; don't bring your chest down to your knees, and don't kick your feet behind you.

Challenge: Once you have mastered the Double Under, try doing a Backwards Double Under. Challenge 2: Add a cross! On the first pass of the rope your arms are open, then cross your arms for the 2nd jump of the Double Under.

Tip: There is no real secret to making the Double Under easier. Just jump higher and spin the rope faster!

Like this:

NOT like this:

EB (or Front Back Cross)

1. Do a Sideswing (page 14) to your left side.

2. While your right arm (still on the left side of your body) continues the up swing, pull your left arm behind your back. Your left hand should be as far to the right side of your back as possible. This will create a loop for you to jump through.

3. After you have jumped through the loop, return your arms to their original sides.

> **Don't forget: this skill can be done to the right side too.**

TS

1. As you jump over the rope, cross your arms behind your back.

2. Keep your arms crossed until after the rope has passed over your head and you've jumped through the loop.

3. Uncross your arms and jump normally.

> **Hint 1:** Your arms should stay close to your back.
> **Hint 2:** The further you cross your arms, the bigger the loop will be for you to jump through.

Harder Tricks

Crougar (aka Leg-over)

1. As you bring the rope over your head, pick up your right leg and hook your right arm underneath it from the inside.

2. Once the rope passes over your head, remove your right arm from under your leg by pulling it into a Sideswing (page 14) on the left side of your body while returning your right foot to the ground.

3. Now bring your right arm back to the right side of your body on the upswing of the rope. Be ready to jump over the rope when it comes around.

Challenge: Once you've mastered the Crougar, try coming out of the leg-over position with a cross. Be sure to cross both arms at the same time! Hint: If you have your right arm under your leg, your right arm will be under your left arm during the cross.

Toad (aka Leg-over Cross)

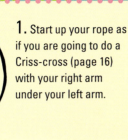

1. Start up your rope as if you are going to do a Criss-cross (page 16) with your right arm under your left arm.

2. With your arms still crossed, lift up your left leg so that it forms a 90° angle with the ground.

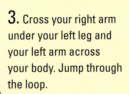

3. Cross your right arm under your left leg and your left arm across your body. Jump through the loop.

Remember: the further you cross your arms, the bigger the loop will be for you to jump through.

4. Once you have jumped over the rope and it has passed over your head, uncross your arms as you would to complete a Criss-cross and jump the rope normally.

AS

1. As you jump over the rope, cross your arms behind your knees.

2. Keep your arms crossed until after you've jumped through the loop.

3. Once you have jumped over the rope, uncross your arms and jump normally.

Hint 1: Your arms should be pressed up against the back of your knees.
Hint 2: The further you cross your arms, the bigger the loop will be for you to jump through.

CL

1. As you jump over the rope, cross one arm behind your knees and the other arm behind your back. Make sure you cross both arms simultaneously.

2. Continue to turn your wrists so that the rope will go around your body. Do not uncross your arms until after you've jumped through the loop.

3. Return your arms to their original sides as you stand up and jump the rope normally.

180°

1. Do a Side-swing (page 14) to your left side.

2. Once the rope hits the ground, immediately turn 180° to your left so that you are facing backward. Jump the rope backwards.

3. After you have jumped the rope and it is on its way to the top of its arc, turn 180° toward the right side so that you are facing the front again and jumping forward.

360°

1. Perform steps 1–2 of the 180°.

2. As soon as you have jumped the rope backwards, complete the 360° rotation by turning a further 180° to your left.

3. You should end up facing the front and jumping forward.

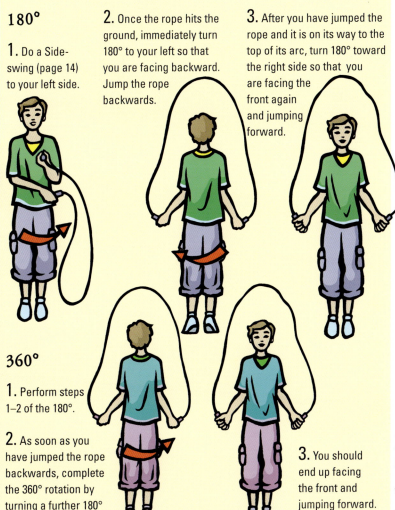

Harder Tricks

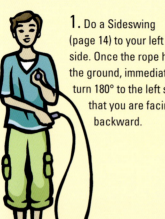

1. Do a Sideswing (page 14) to your left side. Once the rope hits the ground, immediately turn 180° to the left so that you are facing backward.

2. As you bring the rope around to jump it backwards, hook your right arm underneath your right leg from behind. Then jump over the rope.

3. Once the rope has reached the top of its arc, turn 180° to the left so that you are facing forward.

Challenge: Once you are comfortable with the BC, try doing Steps 1 and 2 as a Double Under (page 32)!

4. As you jump over the rope forward, unhook your right arm from under your leg and proceed to jump normally.

Caboose

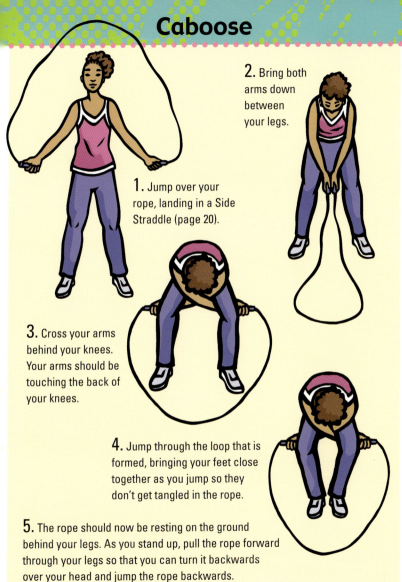

2. Bring both arms down between your legs.

1. Jump over your rope, landing in a Side Straddle (page 20).

3. Cross your arms behind your knees. Your arms should be touching the back of your knees.

4. Jump through the loop that is formed, bringing your feet close together as you jump so they don't get tangled in the rope.

5. The rope should now be resting on the ground behind your legs. As you stand up, pull the rope forward through your legs so that you can turn it backwards over your head and jump the rope backwards.

Mountain Climber

1. Jump over the rope into the Mountain Climber position. This is a modified Push-up (page 44), with your right leg bent so that you can place it halfway between your arms and your feet.

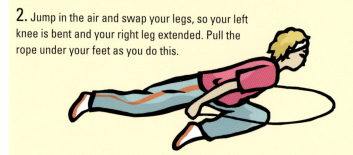

2. Jump in the air and swap your legs, so your left knee is bent and your right leg extended. Pull the rope under your feet as you do this.

3. Repeat Step 1 to switch back to having your right knee bent and your left leg extended.

4. Repeat as many times as you want. Then return to the upright position to jump normally.

Crabs

1. Jump over the rope into a squat position.

2. As you jump over the rope again, extend your left leg in front of you while keeping your right knee bent.

Tip: This trick can be done with the rope turning forwards OR backwards.

3. Pull the rope under you as you switch to having your right leg extended in front of you and your left knee bent.

4. Repeat as many times as you want before returning to the squat position.

5. Return to the upright position to jump normally.

Harder Tricks

Splits

1. Jump over the rope into a squat position.

2. On the next jump of the rope, extend one leg straight in front of you and the other straight behind you so that you land in the Split position. The rope should come to rest in an arc in front of your front foot.

Tip: When landing in the Split position, allow your hands to rest on the ground by your sides for stability.

3. Jump from the Split position to the squat position as you pull the rope under your feet.

Challenge 1: Try doing a Criss-cross (page 16) on the squat jump before the Splits or on the jump coming up from the Splits.

Challenge 2: Try doing 2 Splits in a row! Switch from having your left leg in front to having your right leg in front. Pull the rope under your feet during the switch.

Even Harder Tricks

1. Jump over the rope, landing in a squat position.

2. On the next jump of the rope, extend yourself into the Push-up position with your rope resting in an arc in front of you.

3. Push yourself up off the ground. As soon as you have pushed off with your hands, pull your rope backward so that it slides under your feet as you return to the squat position.

Tip: Push off with both hands and feet at the same time.

Frog

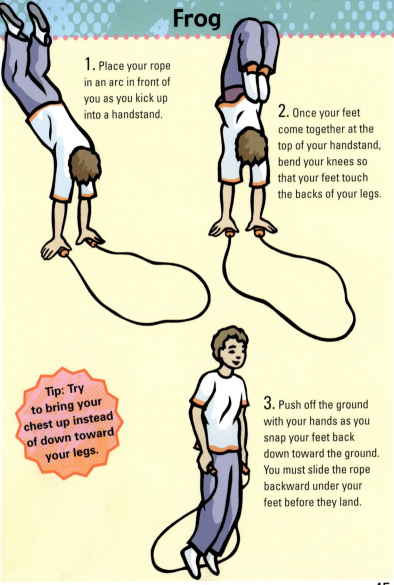

1. Place your rope in an arc in front of you as you kick up into a handstand.

2. Once your feet come together at the top of your handstand, bend your knees so that your feet touch the backs of your legs.

Tip: Try to bring your chest up instead of down toward your legs.

3. Push off the ground with your hands as you snap your feet back down toward the ground. You must slide the rope backward under your feet before they land.

Even Harder Tricks

Triple Unders

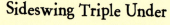

Basic Triple Under

1. Once you jump off the ground, the rope must pass under your feet three times before you land. Remember:

- Spin your wrists in small, fast circles
- Keep your arms close to your body
- Bring your knees up to your chest; don't bring your chest down to your knees and don't kick your feet behind you

Sideswing Triple Under

As with the Basic Triple Under, the rope must make 3 rotations before you land. There are two versions:

Version 1
- Rotation 1: Sideswing to one side
- Rotation 2: Sideswing to the other side
- Rotation 3: Open jump

Version 2
- Rotation 1: Sideswing to one side
- Rotation 2: Open jump
- Rotation 3: Open jump

Sideswing Triple Under with Crosses

Again, once you jump into the air, the rope must make 3 rotations before you land. There are three versions:

Version 1
- Rotation 1: Sideswing to one side
- Rotation 2: Open jump
- Rotation 3: Criss-cross (page 16)

Version 2
- Rotation 1: Sideswing to one side
- Rotation 2: Criss-cross
- Rotation 3: Open jump

Version 3
- Rotation 1: Sideswing to one side
- Rotation 2: Criss-cross
- Rotation 3: Criss-cross

Challenge on version 3: Try switching which arm is crossed on top between rotations 2 and 3.

Awesome Annie

This trick is a combination of the Toad (page 35) and the Crougar (page 34).

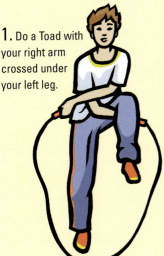

1. Do a Toad with your right arm crossed under your left leg.

2. After you have jumped through the loop and the rope has passed over your head, the following movements must be made simultaneously:
- Uncross your arms
- Jump to place your left leg on the ground and your right leg in front of you at a 90° angle
- Place your right arm under your right leg

3. Once the rope passes over your head again, switch back to the Toad position by executing these steps at the same time:
- Cross your arms so that your right arm is crossed under your left leg again and your left arm is crossed over your body.
- Jump to put your right leg back on the ground and have your left leg in front of you at a 90° angle.

4. Uncross your arms and jump over the rope normally.

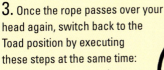

Combination: EB–TS

This trick is a combination of the EB and the TS (page 33).

1. Do an EB with your left arm behind your back and your right arm crossed in front of your body.

2. After you jump the EB, uncross your right arm to bring it to the right side of your body.

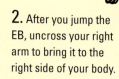

3. As your rope hits the ground to the right side of your body, cross your right arm behind your back so that you are now in the TS position.

4. Jump through the loop while your arms are still crossed behind your back, then uncross your arms so that you can jump normally.

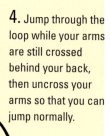

Combination: AS–CL

This trick is a combination of the AS and the CL (page 36).

1. Do an AS with your arms crossed behind your knees.

2. Once you jump through the loop created by the AS, leave the arm that is closest to your legs where it is. Move your other arm up to lie crossed behind your back in the CL position.

3. Jump through the CL loop then uncross your arms and return to the standing position to jump normally.

Leg Cross Triple Unders

Triple Under AS

1. On the first rotation, do a Sideswing (page 14) to one side.

2. Do an open jump on rotation 2. As soon as the rope passes under your feet, begin to cross your arms behind your knees in preparation for the AS (page 36).

3. Rotation 3: AS. Once the rope has passed under your feet to complete the AS, you can uncross your arms and jump normally.

Remember: For any Triple Under, all three rotations of the rope must be completed while you are in the air.

Triple TJ

1. On the first rotation, do a Sideswing to one side.

2. Rotation 2: Toad (page 35) on the same side as the Sideswing. So if you do your Sideswing to the left, you should cross your right arm under your left leg for the Toad.

3. Rotation 3: Open jump.

Hint: On all leg cross multiples, try to bring your legs up instead of throwing your chest down at your legs.

Sideswing Quadruple Under

1. For this skill, once you jump into the air the rope must make *four* rotations before you land. On the first rotation, do a Sideswing (page 14) to one side.

2. Rotation 2: Sideswing to the other side.

3. Rotation 3 and 4: Open jump on both.

EK (360° Triple Under)

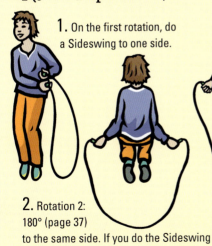

1. On the first rotation, do a Sideswing to one side.

2. Rotation 2: 180° (page 37) to the same side. If you do the Sideswing to the left, you spin 180° to the left while performing the backward jump.

3. Rotation 3: 180°. Once you have brought the rope under your feet backwards in step 2, continue spinning in the same direction, but bring the rope back under your feet in a forward jump. This trick is complete once you are facing forward and the rope has passed under your feet again in the forward direction.

Even Harder Tricks

Frog with a Cross

1. Do steps 1–3 of the Frog (page 45). Once you have pushed off the ground with your hands, pull your arms back with a Criss-cross (page 16).

2. Slide your crossed rope under your feet before they touch the ground.

AS–Pushup

1. Do steps 1–3 of the AS (page 36). As you jump the loop formed from the AS, extend out into the Push-up position (page 44).

2. Slide the rope under your feet as your jump to the squat position from the Push-up.

3. An AS–Splits is performed in the same way, substituting the Splits (page 42) for the Push-up.

Pushup with a Cross

1. Do steps 1–3 of the Push-up (page 44). Once you have pushed off the ground with your hands, pull your arms back with a Criss-cross (page 16).

2. Slide your crossed rope under your feet before they touch the ground.

Frog–AS

1. Do steps 1–3 of the Frog (page 45). Once you have pushed off the ground with your hands, pull your arms straight backward to slide the rope under your feet before they land.

2. Immediately after the rope passes under your feet, cross your arms behind your legs in the AS position (page 36).

3. Jump the AS, then uncross your arms and return to a standing position to jump normally.

Split–Pushup

1. Jump over the rope into the Splits position (page 42).

2. Jump from the Splits into the Push-up position, whipping the rope under your feet between the two skills.

3. Slide the rope under your feet as you jump to the squat position from the Push-up.

Partner Skills

Basic Scoop

1. A 'Scoop' is a general term used to describe a jump in which you are using your rope to jump or 'scoop' another person. It is important that you and your partner are 100% in sync. Start by jumping next to your partner.

2. Jump to the side to align yourself behind your partner.

Challenge: Also try aligning yourself in front of your partner to perform the scoop.

3. Both you and your partner must now jump over the rope. You should be close behind your partner so that you do not have to stretch to complete the scoop.

Hint: It is easiest to scoop your partner if you keep the rope moving slowly. Once you have mastered the technique, then you can try to scoop faster.

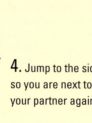

4. Jump to the side so you are next to your partner again.

Scoops with Footwork

1. Align yourself behind or in front of your partner.

2. While you are both jumping over the rope, try performing the following footwork skills:
- Skier (page 19)
- Bell (page 19)
- Side Straddle (page 20)
- Forward Straddle (page 20)
- Jogging Step (page 22)
- Hopscotch (page 23)
- Swing Kick (page 23)
- Can-can (page 21)
- Heel-to-toe (page 24)
- Fling (page 24)
- Russian Cossack (page 25)
- Spread Eagle (page 25)
- Cross Over (page 26)

Scoop with Swing Kick

Scoop with Skier

Hint:
If you are positioned behind your partner, you may need to alter your footwork positioning slightly so that you do not kick your partner in front of you. You can kick slightly to the side of your partner.

Partner Skills

1. In this trick, the partner holding the rope (the 'scooper') should do a 180° turn (page 37) toward the partner who is being scooped (the 'scoopee'). Begin by standing side-by-side with your partner.

2. Start the 180° by doing a Sideswing (page 14) to your side between you and the scoopee.

3. Move straight into the 180° from the Sideswing. Once the rope has passed over your head, jump so that you are positioned directly in front of the scoopee. You should now be face to face with each other.

4. Complete the 180° with a Backward Jump that will pass under you and the scoopee.

5. Take a Backward Jump as you move to the side of the scoopee.

Sideswing Scoop

This skill can be done from either side. For the sake of clarity, I will explain it with the scooper on the right side.

1. Position yourselves so that you, the scooper, are on the right side. Do a Sideswing (page 14) on your right side, which is the side away from the scoopee.

2. Bring both arms over to your left side on the next rotation of the rope, so that your left arm is closest to your left side and your right arm reaches across the front of your partner's body. This should form a loop through which your partner can jump.

3. Swing the rope so that it clears your partner's head. Next, bring your right arm back to your right side so you can normally.

Sideswing Scoop with Power

Sideswing Scoop with Pushup or Split

1. Scooper: follow the instructions for the Sideswing Scoop (page 57). Scoopee: while the scooper does the Sideswing away from you, do a squat jump.

2. Scoopee: when the loop comes around which the scooper has made for you, jump through it into the Push-up (shown here) or Split (page 42) position.

3. Return to the squat position, then to the standing position as the scooper resumes normal jumping.

Sideswing Scoop with Frog

1. Scooper: follow the instructions for the Sideswing Scoop (page 57).

2. Scoopee: when the loop comes around which the scooper has made for you, dive through it, hands first, into the Frog position (page 45).

3. Snap down to your feet and continue jumping as the scooper resumes normal jumping.

Push-up Scoop

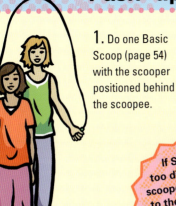

1. Do one Basic Scoop (page 54) with the scooper positioned behind the scoopee.

2. On the second jump, the scoopee does a squat jump.

If Step 4 is too difficult, the scooper can move to the side of the scoopee's Push-up and continue jumping.

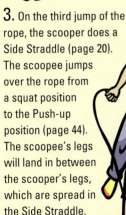

3. On the third jump of the rope, the scooper does a Side Straddle (page 20). The scoopee jumps over the rope from a squat position to the Push-up position (page 44). The scoopee's legs will land in between the scooper's legs, which are spread in the Side Straddle.

4. On the fourth turn of the rope, the scoopee jumps from the Push-up position over the rope to the squat position.

Partner Skills

One Wheel or 2-in-1

1. Stand next to your partner, facing forward. Each of you should be holding one handle of the rope. Hold the handle in the hand that is furthest from your partner.

2. Bring the rope around so that you can both do a Basic Jump just as if one person was holding both ends of the rope.

It is very important that you and your partner are turning the rope at the same time and jumping at the same time.

3. You can vary this by having one person jump the rope while the other partner stands to the side and helps turn the rope. Take turns switching between being the jumper and the turner.

Footwork

1. While you are jumping over the rope, try performing some footwork skills:

- Skier (page 19)
- Bell (page 19)
- Side Straddle (page 20)
- Forward Straddle (page 20)
- Jogging Step (page 22)
- Hopscotch (page 23)
- Swing Kick (page 23)
- Can-can (page 21)
- Heel-to-toe (page 24)
- Fling (page 24)
- Russian Cossack (page 25)
- Spread Eagle (page 25)
- Cross Over (page 26)

Double Under

Try this first with one person jumping and the other helping to turn. Once you are able to do the Double Under with one person, try with both partners in the rope.

1. Give a 'Ready, Set, Go' call. On the jump after 'Go', the jumper should jump extra high. Both partners must turn the rope fast enough to pass under the jumper's feet twice before he or she lands.

One Wheel with Can-can

Cross

1. One person jumps and the other helps to turn the rope. Give a 'Ready, Set, Go' call. On the count after 'Go', the jumper crosses their outside arm across their body. At the same time the turner, with the rope in their outside hand, crosses their arm on top of the jumper's arm across the jumper's body to form a cross.

2. Both people should uncross on the next turn of the rope.

Partner Skills

Traveller

Basic Traveller

1. One person – the traveller – will have a rope. Everyone should line up in a straight line, arm-distance apart. The traveller stands at one end of the line, facing the others in the line.

2. The traveller begins to jump Basic Bounces while moving toward the first person in the line. Everyone in line jumps at the same time, holding their arms to their sides, behind their backs, or on their stomachs.

3. The traveller performs a Basic Scoop (pg 54) on the first person in the line. After one jump with the first scoopee, the traveller moves to the gap between the first two people in the line and jumps a Basic Bounce.

4. The traveller scoops everyone in the line, taking one or two jumps between each person.

> Traveller can be done with any number of people.

Traveller Variations

Shotgun

1. Everyone lines up in a straight line, elbow-distance apart, with the traveller at one end of the line. The traveller performs a Basic Scoop (page 54) on the first person in the line. Without taking a jump between people, the traveller must move directly from scooping the first person to scooping the next person in line. Continue this pattern until you have scooped the final person in the line. If you have six jumpers in your line, it should only take the traveller six jumps to reach the end of the line.

Weave

1. Arrange the jumpers in a staggered line with every other person positioned two steps forward. The traveller will move in the lane between the two lines, scooping the first person from the front then the next person from behind, alternating until the end of the line.

Pairs and Triples Scoops

1. Instead of only scooping one person at a time, try scooping two or three people that are lined up directly in front of one another. Make sure you stay close, jump high, and jump at the same time! When scooping three people, you may prefer to arrange them in a triangle formation.

Split

1. Each jumper in the line forms a pair with the person next to them. The taller person stands about one step behind the shorter person. There must be enough space between the 2 paired jumpers for the traveller to pass through. The traveller then scoops both members of the pair at the same time, before moving on to the next pair.

Index of Tricks